It's a Shark!

Practicing the SH Sound

Amber King

Rosen
PHONICS
READERS

Rosen
Classroom™

I swim in the ocean.
What is that shadow?

It is a shark!
I know all about sharks.

Sharks shoot through water.

Sharks come in many shapes.
This whale shark is big!

Some sharks have sharp teeth.

This shark shows its teeth.
They are sharp!

This turtle has a shell.
Some sharks bite through shells.